How Love Begins

Poetry & Prose To Reignite Your Passion for Love

Book: Liam Xavier

Cover: Sigourney Whitesel

Editing: Lauren Cresswell

Other work by Liam Xavier:

Writer:

Whispers to The World (2018)

Welcome to Hell (2020)

Co-*Editor (With Max Moore)*

Oh, To Be Young Again - Ken Wiffen (2021)

Contents

To every Love that left me with a lesson. Thank you.

Introduction

This book is one of those projects that exists in divine timing. I am a fickle creative who works on multiple projects at the same time regularly, but this one was always hidden from view. I would write poems and letters to Loved ones, but be too nervous to ever show them. This book began to write itself and come together as soon as I understood what Love meant a little clearer and as soon as I began to mature my train of thought.

For those who know me, they know I have been less than lucky when it comes to romantic endeavours or rather they've been complicated. But as such, stories build and lessons are learnt which may hurt as heartbreak but are wonderful as inspiration. I could continue to write of the pain, of the hurt, of the miscommunication, or of the unreturned Love, but that's not how I feel anymore. Nor is it the whole truth. Over years of falling for people, my perception has evolved - my lifelong fascination with the subject of Love continues but now I focus less on the negatives. Love is far more expansive than that. While it is true that some are just blatantly bad for us and there is no justification for a thing that is eating away at our soul, Love generally comes with some really beautiful moments.

This book is for those moments. This book is a collection of my own personal mementos from Loves confessed, Loves bottled up, Loves shared and more. It is a gift shop of romantic souvenirs that asks you to read through and find yourself in their stories. Once you have, let it remind you that Love and everything that comes with it will always be worth falling back into. This book is for everyone who needs a reason to believe in Love again.

My last two books have just been poetry, but I wanted to change that for this book. Love can be expressed in so many different ways and there is so much that can and should be said. So in the first 3 sections, you will see a collection of poetry, themed around different feelings and questions regarding Love. In the final section, you will see a selection of personal essays, similar to those I've written for publications like Thought Catalog, Unwritten and Be A Light. Obviously, I hope you read the whole book but I've created this format in the hopes that there will be something in here for everyone, so when you feel sad you can come back here and use one of the poems or essays as reference. Use it in the way that works best for you. Welcome to How Love Begins. Settle in, grab a hot drink and fall in Love with Love all over again.

Part 1: the poems

Prologue poem

This book in creation was one of staggered patience;

A rag tag bunch of poetic excitations, chaotically collated

in notepad pages, chronicling changing stages which never made

sense when read together until I found the tether,

as light as feather but as strong as steel.

A book, so divine in conscious timing that my mind

set its sights on starting as soon as the feeling struck.

Because, you see, this book is about Love.

My heart had never felt ready to steady its shaking hand enough to

tell it's story and I had not found the maturity

to procure the assurety of what Love was to me.

Then a box appeared with a bow and string,

to bring me what I needed to know:

the glow of gifted beauty;

the patience of precious angels,

the Love of purest Loves that sunk the rotting ship of its

bitter shoulder sitting chip.

I listened to the signs and let my sorrows go

and upon their exit, I gained a fresh perspective

on life's enlightening journey

and set pen to paper once again

bringing these old inked friends of mine together,

in a way I never imagined.

Crafting new odes to clarity,

opening my eyes to the true vastness of Love,

to the understanding now in my heart

that I once thought far too black and white

and now dream in colours undefined

without the need for a palette.

Colours that merge into each other with no name,

colours that paint the sky with brush strokes

only seen by those that listen to the shean

of their infinite intimacy.

This book in creation was written,

arranged, edited and Loved

at a time when my mind

knew of its capabilities

and of the passionate potential pouring from my soul,

of the whole heavenly elicitation of healing sensations.

This is to say, I wrote this book with a smile,

knowing Love is not just about the people.

It's not just about the highs or lows

but it's about those tongue tickling questions

that like a trick candle keep burning inside of us,

to sustain the flame in our stomachs.

To tie all experiences together in silk string and ribbon

to remind us that it's always a gift.

To dance upon a chance and feel blessed by its existence.

To write a book of poems,

young and old, and to know how they speak,

loud and momentous when placed together,

giving new hope to oft' hurt hearts

that there is beauty in starting over.

After all that is **How Love**,

in all its forms, **Begins**.

Chapter 1: the fascination of infatuation

Before anything comes a period of intrigue, fascination and infatuation. The point at which we realise there is more to a person than being a stranger, or simply someone we vaguely know. A point at which a person intrigues us and sparks a feeling in us so indefinable that we can do nothing but find out what it means. A point at which that feeling has yet to establish or name itself as Like, Lust, Love or something entirely undiscovered.

We have to get a taste.

We have to learn more about them, more about the connection we have with them. The things they Love and the things we have in common with them. Every poem in this chapter explores *the fascination of infatuation*. Those moments where our brains are alive with the drug of discovery. Those moments where we meet someone new and have yet to find out where they fit in our lives. A moment so impossibly interesting that we desire so often to find that feeling again.

Now is your chance to relive that feeling and as you do, think of who comes to mind and forget how your relationship with them might have ended. Sink into a space, protected by the walls of this book and remind yourself how it feels to feel so enamoured with the prospect of someone new.

Peace in simplicity

You give me something I didn't think to look for.

Colours in practice

Even if it were pitch black,

I would still be able to see the vibrancy of our Love,

Because ours is not one painted with colours

Just for the eyes, unable to see at night.

Ours is armed with a palette made for the body;

The head and the mind inside it,

The arms,

The organs,

The skin,

The muscle,

The hairs,

The stretch marks,

The joints,

The places we forget exist,

The little details that define us.

Ours is a Love that paints a sky,

But not the type to be found in the atmosphere of a planet

But the type that has no boundaries

Between the earth and universe.

Ours is all the colours of life,

Seen, felt, heard and tasted.

Let me always be a kind of memory

List me in the names you will never forget,
no matter what.

Constellation

As we sit here, with the countryside as our universe

and you cocooned in the nook between my chest and arm,

waiting for a time when you feel safe to emerge a butterfly,

please notice the stars.

Notice the moon and sky,

even the tender touch of the winter wind.

Notice that you, that we, are here amongst it all.

Notice how the ticking taunt of time evaporates

with the sweeping sounds of a sleeping sunrise.

Notice the feeling in your heart; notice the beating.

I know it hurts sometimes but when it does,

come back to me and breathe it all in.

We'll escape to the place where time stops

and I want you to know that even in the cocoon,

you are the butterfly.

In the making

Some feelings absorb you in such a way
that your pen wants to write of nothing else
until it finds the perfect poem.

Siren

The world loses its solidity in her presence,
a melting fondue
it drips off the surface and becomes a malleable
mouth watering delicacy.
Open the mind and find the door to Narnia.
a dream state of foundations awake,
a moreish medication to tease the brain
into a welcome resuscitation.
Spark that most insatiable radiation and feel the heart fly
like the wind was made to carry it.
Listen to the soul cry out with satisfaction
like music was made to hear it.
What symphonic serenity sung with rarity;
a lost chord plucked by its discoverer.
No ears can find their way back to a monotone melody
once she has shown them her siren song.

Your certainty

I want to be the one you tell stories about,

the name you Love to drop into conversation

like you have never been certain of Love before.

Llike each time you think of me, you have to skip and dance

because happiness is such an infectious melody.

And your happiness would be my greatest goal.

Lusting

Your hope is not lost,
it's just lusting over the thought of Love.
It's getting distracted, looking for loopholes,
caught up in a corner facing a plaster wall,
just waiting to break through it.
Trust in its timing.
Time is lost when rushed and time after time
your hope will remind you that it was never gone;
just out searching for better things.

Simple pleasures

Everything is better with a little sunshine,
a couple of drinks and a fleeting moment
of summer freedom.

Think less, feel more

I say

"There is no way out of this"

You say

"Life is not so logical, my dear. Wait a little longer, I promise.

Wait and listen closely."

Burning

There is little in pen or pencil,

in air or fire,

that can describe

this total desire

for your Love.

No turning back now

She utters a phrase so sweet
and my skin begins to lift
and my mind begins to fluster
and my heart, he sings to me:
"Brother, we are in trouble."

Leave it to the cold sea

Swim with me at night,

when the cold touch obscures our peripheral sight.

The waves will be calm and our hands will intertwine,

bloodied palm against bloodied palm.

And upon seeing your face,

I will imagine the crashing of china plates,

as my heart falls for your wistful grace.

Fearful as the sun losing the day,

I would hold you, head against chest,

and wish for you to stay.

But if my heart can beat as fast as it does

and if yours beats the same,

then maybe, just maybe, Love will find Love.

Awash

Your touch cleanses and all becomes clear.
Your Love is a baptism of serenity & peace.

Still here

When the lights are low and my candles burn slow,
I can feel her in the atmosphere.
As if the universe could connect our two souls
from miles apart, through the flickering of a burning wick.
As if her hand was here touching the hairs of my chest
and my arm around her shoulder and our breaths
exhaling into the same air.

Flutters

Even today, you smile
and the butterflies begin their little dance.
That first smile that cocooned sweet caterpillars
and the same one that gave them wings.

Never bored in your company

I could listen to you for hours,

your voice,

your thoughts,

even your silence.

So long as I am there and so are you

and our energy lives with tenderness,

then I could not care less about what we do.

Your sky as well as mine

With both eyes I observe your sky from miles away.

I regard the distant stars,

impatient to break through,

I note the tiniest details and envision you doing the same.

I paint a picture of our two bodies, touching arms,

sunken into the grass of the fields,

with eyes fixated on the sky

but energies connected by our sides.

Just by sharing the same clouds, I can feel you beside

and my frown softens and my smile widens.

I miss you and I don't,

because you are here watching the sky;

the same one as mine.

Nature Knows Best

I found Love when I told the trees about you
and even they – in all their magnificence –
could not help but to blush at the idea of your radiance.

In your own time

I know it is not my place to make you see what I can;

that I must give you an idea

so you may gently believe it yourself,

but some days, I wish I could remove my brain

and feed it into a TV projector,

just so, for one day at least, you could see it all.

Something new

There are so many stories behind your eyes
that I am dying to find the keys to.

I understand it now

Of all the years of falling,
I have been making room
in this cluttered little heart
for a Love just like yours.

Learning in practice.

Through you, I learnt what I needed
to be truly true to myself.

Tell me everything

Let me learn about you through your fears.

Through your belief or disbelief in a God,

Through your happiest memory and your saddest.

Through a tour of your physical scars.

Through a discussion into political passion.

After all, what have we ever learnt

from simple polite small talk?

More than beauty

I still remember the day I saw you,

infatuated by beauty,

soon to be enamoured by intelligence.

Chosen to unite a 2nd time

The chances of us being alive individually
are 1 in 400 trillion and yet here we are.
So imagine the chances of us being alive,
side by side in the same world,
in the same universe, and yet here we are.
This connection is a selection from our divine angels,
our guardians, smiling to themselves on the day
we were born, knowing we were babies
that did not know the diamonds we would discover.
Our guardians that guarded this precious peaceful Masterpiece until
the day our energies found a destiny,
a recipe for cheaper therapy
where the question of our social alienation
was answered by the presence
of a lens that looked through our souls
and found a reflection.
In my own mirror, I see myself
as a beautiful entity of brilliance,
but when we speak, I am seen in a way
I did not think was possible.
In the same way I have bloodied my hands

giving my heart and whole being

to others for them to see,

you have found the blue in my eyes and understood it all.

It is a mental massage to think of this journey,

the creation of a Love laced collective,

carefully curated by spiritual patience.

This chamomile, ocean water fragrance

that sprays its sensual sensation

and leaves our hearts in a state of earthly elation.

For all the breaking of my body,

I have been guided back to a point of rebirth

where I have met you anew.

Hello again, it is nice to meet you.

Let me learn about what life looks like in your eyes,

let me bear witness to your evolution as I continue mine.

Let me introduce myself,

with a mind you have not known before.

Let us soar through the air with eyes closed

like we have no need for wings to fly,

like the sky can be accessed without the need for planes,

like all the pains we have experienced

cause no harm in this existence.

Let us believe in the almighty potential of a miraculous Being,

as we teach each other of things

that settle our spiritual hunger so that as we grow older,

our souls are always younger in energy.

Even if we just become each others memory

of a time gone by,

let us smile and breathe for a while

and hold onto this iridescent essence of universal heaven.

Infatuation

It may sound terribly cliché
but those blue eyes
were a perfect reflection of her kindness;
that smile was a gift
to her atmosphere.

In The Quiet of An Evening

Run your hands through my hair
as I lean against your leg,
open and vulnerable,
softened and soothed,
calmed and full of Love.
Delicately play with these curls
and send me to sleep.
I could stay like this forever.
Let the moon rise and the sun fall,
let the sun rise and the moon fall.
So long as your small hands
are massaging my skull,
time will not matter.

No words need be spoken

This beautiful silence
holds our two hearts,
perfectly at peace.

Supernova Sentiments

I think I finally know
why the stars shine
the way they do
when we are watching;
not for me,
not for you,
but for the gap in between
that keeps us listening.

I still ask - to remember what it's like to care enough

Your Love
encourages me
to ask questions,
purely for the fascination
of asking,
whatever the answer may be.
Even when there is no answer to find.

Cared for ourselves first

I am glad

we learnt how to be alone,

rather than

diving into each other

without a care

for the damage we could cause.

Pure Love Preservation

Take my hand
and I promise,
I will only let go
if the grip
becomes too tight
and our paths divulge
too far apart.
I will only let go
if to open my hand
and watch you walk away
is the kindest way
to keep you close.
For if Love exists
only from a distance,
to still see you
and Love you, a kind of way,
would be better than
gripping too tight
to a Love that wants to go.

Few people

Few people in my life
will ever come close
to the magnificent magnitude of you.

Following the feeling, without force.

Magnetic is the feeling,
so unfamiliar
and yet persuasive in its pull.

More to know

Catch me eye-to-eye

with sudden silence;

your mystery is sweet violence

to my anxious compliance.

You make me squint

for more information

that sparks an elation,

hidden behind a dumbfounded

complacency of heart.

You are a piece of gallery art

that asks that you look a little closer,

before being worthy of

its rawest beauty.

Chapter 2: What is Love? The Ultimate Question

Naturally, you can't write a book about Love without at least broaching the conversation around what exactly it is. Yet, the conversation will never be a finished or concrete one and the answer is as broad and as complex as the answer to how big the galaxy is. So the only way we can really approach the answer is from a subjective point of view. Fundamentally, Love is subjective anyway. It is a highly personal, prone to change, feeling. It is a birdsong in the morning. It is silence in the evening. It is the sound of a babbling brook. It is the sight of a Loved one who has been gone for months on end.

With such a subjective, evolving feeling, we have the ability, in poetry, to put words and images to that expanse. We are able to find a channel to which the blood of romance and infatuation runs through into ink. It is everything as dramatic as that and everything as simple as understanding that your heart beats faster when they walk close by. However, whatever I say in this introduction, whatever poems exist in this section, Love will change again. For me. For you. For all of us. We will relate one day and not another. We will believe it to be one thing, and then contradict that thought just a week later. In fact, one of the most beautiful, defining elements of Love and our true, endearing perception of it is that it's power and impact is neither finite nor fixed. It is moveable. Malleable. Flowing. So what is it to you? Right now. Today. This second?

As you read this next chapter's poems, ask yourself if you agree with any of them. If the description feels personal to *you*. Equally, if you don't agree, use this chapter to think of how you might summarise it or how you believe it feels when *you* are experiencing its touch. Like I said, this book is much an exercise in self-reflection as it is an object of entertainment. This is your chance to delve into one of the most debated questions of our lives and approach it with utter excitement and joy.

To Love is to keep your expectations high

I grew up on 90s and naughties rom-com corniness,

Nora Ephron and Nicholas Sparks,

midnight kisses and destined hearts,

chance encounters and serendipity.

Not taking anything too literally,

but it set the tone for the way in which the Love I've known

has grown inside of me.

The way in which the soil has nurtured a seed

and grown a tree.

So it was no surprise when, as my eyes began

to expand in size at the prospect of love at first sight,

that those around me began to tell me

to lower my expectations; to drop my standards a little bit,

because life is not made of fairy tales and miracles

and that as I got older,

I would realise there are compromises we must make.

But with each year,

I only fell more in love with the idea of what I needed,

not what I wanted,

nor even the image I imagined people thought

I saw,

but the connection and attention to detail

that my heart calls for.

Because I have already defied expectation in this life,

I rose up from the ground, a phoenix and became the miracle

so, I have already removed the word impossible

from my vocabulary.

And, no, I am not naive to the fact that I am a textbook Freudian

case, where I was denied love as a child

and now find it in others,

but that does not change the state of Love I dream of.

It does not make it any more unachievable,

so sit back and watch as I describe a Love

that my body and mind aches for.

Read my words, and think of your own.

My Love is a soft kiss amongst sunset bliss.

My Love is a glass of white wine under a starry sky.

My Love is a trip abroad to a country

we've never even heard of.

My Love is a phone call in which I can feel us, side by side.

My Love is the oxytocin high of touching skin.

My Love is affection and protection without dependence.

My love is sharing anecdotes about work

and watching the passion behind our eyes.

My Love is believing in more,

it is understanding that the world is in existence,

that we are bones and muscle that know how to speak,

that know how to hold each other just right,

how to put words to feeling,

how to put feeling to action,

how to Love with all our bodies brilliance.

My Love is my dream, but by no means unreal,

because I have already felt moments in which

my mind sits up to attention.

I have already painted my heart with the experience

of romantic consciousness.

My Love is not a silly movie that's fun to watch.

My Love is not imagination taken too far.

My Love is not even high standards.

My Love is just swimming through the tide

of Loves many currents and knowing as I go,

which one crashes me against the rocks

and which takes me to shore.

I may not know my Love yet, but I have known a version,

And when my Love arrives,

I will be glad that I took the time to get to know myself first.

To Love is to smile a little longer

I Love to Love;

to discover another from the surface of their beauty

to the depths of their soul,

to the education of their influence.

The inference that there is more to

the world than our reality,

this disruption of banality,

the shout of profanity when there are no other words

to describe the moment: *"FUCK"*

you have sunken into the sand of their shoes.

I even Love the wars battled upon the heartbreak happening

in crowds of claustrophobia.

Even the moments that don't feel

like moments worth remembering.

Because the course of Love never did run smooth

but it does sand down the rougher edges of my heart.

And with every start is a serotonin injection.

And with every end is the promise of finding another.

So I shall put one foot in front of the other

and believe in the path I follow,

regardless of how many dead-ends I encounter.

Perfection Changes

Like Love itself, you soon realise that

the 'perfect poem' changes each time you write a line.

It grows, it evolves, it moves in time with strings of violins

and morphs until you are discovering an entirely new act

of being, with each new poem and person.

You realise that Love & poetry are never truly finished,

but rather,

they are infinite,

paired hand in hand,

with the vast boundlessness of the cosmos.

Strings & violins

There is nothing more beautiful than finally realising that the heart
was never meant to beat BECAUSE of someone,
nor FOR them,
but in time with them -
and that is the real music of life.

An Ocean

At first glance, love is an ocean -

a vast expanse of beauty and feeling,

deeper than the eyes can see.

But really, love is more than just a single ocean -

it is the crashing plates

beneath the Tsunami disasters they create

and then it is a small ladybird or an English oak.

It is the universe, it is Mars

and every suggestion of a life without confirmation.

It is a formation of stars with no name.

It is the exploding sun,

the silent darkness, the black hole

the Gods of greek history and the devils of Christian myth.

You see, at first glance, Love is an ocean,

but on further inspection,

an ocean barely covers a first kiss.

Coming Home

Love is not a concept saved for just a few,
Love is an experience of everything and everyone -
a taste of the world's population
centred on the lips of a Lover.
Love is the midnight train with no tracks to follow
but the light of the moon.
Love is coming home to a home you didn't even realise
was yours to come home to,
but one that felt so perfectly familiar.
Love is finding the bricks and then watching a house be built
before you even remember how.
Love is feeling a comfort so soft it tickles the tongue
like cotton candy.
Love is a word without definition
and a feeling without bounds.
Love is everything we know it to be
and so much more, undiscovered.

Prepared Pt.1

When we are ready to be Loved,

we will find Love in a purer form.

We will open our arms to the warm comfort

of a diamond desire

and feel the shine of its jewel

hang round our necks,

decorating our skin

with a devoted notion of honesty

and compassion.

When are ready to be Loved,

it will appear, as though it was always there,

under the nose

and just out of reach of the eyes.

Prepared Pt. 2

When we are ready to be Loved
and be Loved with the whisper of every hair on our body
and be Loved by our own hearts call as much as our Lovers,
We will know how to receive Love.
We will know how to treat it,
how to believe it
and how to keep it in our souls
even when it must go.

Rhymes

Love was born of the poet's mind
and finds itself intertwined with the heart
and all the senses.
I feel the emptiness of lost space,
I see the vision of a fading face,
I smell the perfume left on my jumpers,
I hear the happiness of solemn summers,
I taste the bitterness of times mistress,
but I do not fight them,
I write them into rhymes designed to shine a light.

Beyond what we know

I imagine to answer the question of Love,

we must transcend into the farthest universe from our own,

so that our mind can lose its attachment to antiquated ideals.

I imagine drifting between burning stars

and floating dust clouds and breathing in matter

until my breath can speak of Love so freshly.

To be an alien to my own world and watch without the

words of conservative teachers to broaden my mind

and merely hold Love,

hear Love,

feel Love

as an essence,

as a being,

as an object,

as a universal anomaly,

and to let it baptise me where I stand.

I imagine to answer the question of Love,

we have to first forget everything and start over

with intuition and instinct.

Rushed

We are too impatient with Love,

we hold the prospect of its power in our hands like a hot pan.

We grab it with bare hands straight from the oven,

we do not give ourselves the chance

to enjoy the taste without pain.

We run after it without looking at our surroundings

and trip up and hit the sand.

We turn the page before

we've had a chance to read the words,

We close our eyes and wait for daylight

without stopping to watch the stars at night.

But, my dear friends,

the wait,

the patience,

to take our time

gifts a beautiful journey

surpassing any we've been on yet.

Lines upon my palm

With each Loves hand,

I learn that Love, in its purest form,

Is an evolving amalgamation of undefined experiences.

It is lines running along our palms,

waiting to be translated

into stories.

Up next

Sometimes the destiny is not them,
but what they lead you to.

Simply Complex

Love is knowing when it feels wrong enough to leave.

Love is knowing when it feels good enough to stay.

Love is knowing it's never as simple as that,

but knowing you'd never want it to be.

Sweet addiction

Love is taking a bite of a ripe peach,

feeling the bristle of its hairs on your bright cheek

and being so consumed by the sweetness of its juice,

that it drips down the lips and has you drooling for more.

Dreaming

Love sings a full set of a concert

without ever needing anyone to watch.

Love is a young girl singing into her hairbrush

and being happier than she's ever been.

Love is falling to sleep

and having no doubt,

that you will dream

in some of the brightest colours that exist,

and knowing that you deserve

every single one as a portrait of your own passion.

Freeflow

Love is writing a poem and letting the words flow,
like they had been waiting all year to sing.
Love is reading back the lyrics
and not knowing where they came from,
but knowing that they still feel
electric.

When there are no words

Love is finding every synonym that exists in your vocabulary

and still never truly saying anything

accurate enough to describe the feeling.

It is finding nonsense words and noises

and smells

and tastes

and sounds

and sights

that make more sense than any word leaving the mouth.

It is these poems, creating worlds in your mind.

It is them reaching every sense as evidence

that you still remember the feeling.

It is you (hopefully) smiling because you remember.

It is you thinking not of the words, but of the feeling.

Butterfly

(Inspired by a prompt by Jasmine S. Higgins)

I think we got it wrong
by describing butterflies in the stomach.
I think if we were telling the truth,
we would say that their smile & voice
gives us a hiccup in the throat
& a sugar-rush palpitation in the heart
that seems to last for 4 hours and 38 minutes.
I think we would say
that their laugh, their nose & their name
curls our toes to scrape the carpet
& leaves the legs all dead and tingly
until Love looks like a limp.
I think we would be better off saying
that it gives us static in our hair
until their hands are running through it.
That it looks like bitten nails after
an over-thought text message,
that it is the image of a whole wildlife sanctuary in the mind;
with roars from lions & flying eagles
& giraffes that still look like dinosaurs to me.
& yes, a few butterflies too
but I guess, a butterfly stomach
just rolls off the tongue a little easier.

Love is a God without a name

Listen to the gospel of infinite galaxies.
Listen to the Love blushing from the tops of trees.
Listen to the choir of our solar counsel.
Listen now, to my testimony to the stars, to the universe,
to everything that fills me with connection,
to everything I sit down and pray to in the morning,
to everything I access with legs crossed and a mind open,
to the roots between my feet and this world,
from my skull to the sky.
I am the shadow of a semi-Christian beginning,
and now my God is everywhere.
He is not a man looking down on all of us,
he's not a He or a She or anything other than an essence.
My agnostic God is a contradiction only when explained
and it was never meant for explanation in the first place.
My God is the grass on my back in the Summer,
my God is the sudden spirit
that lifts me back from depression,
My God is the faceless beauty that I notice in another's eyes,
my God is the infinity of happiness
when I feel Love so timeless
that even the clock stops counting.
My God cannot be found in just one book,
but in all of them
and in the experience of reading, itself.
My God is the saviour that does not stop us
acknowledging our own strength,

my God allows us to carve our own path,
while giving us the resource of Fate
to know all decisions are divine.
My God has been found
through the resuscitation of my rapture;
a pleasure of presence that gifted me a present of inquisition,
a loss of precision and
a widened vision.
My new religion questions itself
and finds more to Love every day.
My new religion does not discredit yours
because it understands that none us will ever understand
what life planned for our birth,
nor what it has yet to plan for our death.
And if you and I both pray in different ways,
to different things but still come out of it
more hopeful and heartened, then I have no business caring
whose name you call when you clasp your hands
to honour them.
My new religion has risen my soul from its sombre state
and given new celebration to these eyes opening
to see the sun through the cracks in my curtains,
to the baptism of my burdens when I take a notepad and pen
to the lake and immerse my worst thoughts
into the force of visceral verse.
So listen to the Gospel of Infinite Galaxies.
Listen to the Love blushing from the tops of trees.
Listen to the choir of our Solar Counsel.
Listen now, to my testimony to the Stars, to The Universe,

and understand just a little better
why I am able to find a way to smile,
when even the muscles in my mouth do not understand
their own existence.
Understand that I am also just a man,
questioning his life,
without the need for any answers.
I am a Being,
in Love with believing
in More.

Chapter 3: Upon Reflection

I know this is a chapter but really 'Upon Reflection' could very well be an alternative name for this whole book. It's the whole point. I am only able to write this book because the majority of events these poems are about have passed and I am reflecting on their existence. It's funny, isn't it? How things change when we've had the chance to breathe, to grieve, to leave. It's funny how suddenly, after a year or 2 passes, we start to see things from a place of clarity and can look back with a softer touch.

We can remember the utter beauty that was afforded to us and understand that a lot of us are just making mistakes and trying to learn how to live life, messily. So I think – given we're talking about general people and not utter twats – it's important to look back on old situations, especially romantic ones. It's important to change our lenses and see where each has impacted us on the journey we are now on. It's important to use these experiences to forgo the need for a 'forever' person, or at least the desperate pain of expecting someone new to leave you at any point. It's important to know that at different stages of our lives, we evolve and at these stages, we don't always align with the same people we once did. It's important to look back and wonder what more can be learnt, **upon reflection.**

Kindness

I stuck to you like string cheese to the roof of the mouth:

a flavour with great taste at its core,

but a nuisance for both involved.

I was finding sweet school-time infatuation

at the centre of your eyes;

a fantasy of an adult life at just sixteen.

I was a boy caught up, but really

I was a boy, lonely

and you were a girl, with kindness.

And though it felt more like a shattering, clattering

world record Love inside of me,

I was really just grateful to be privy to such friendship.

To be given a chance by someone who had no need

to offer for me anything, and that is the real

sticky substance of the situation; the honey to the tongue,

the kindness never forgotten.

The first girl

You were the first girl I believe I ever Loved.

Goodness knows I'm not sure I even knew what Love was

to call it such a thing but you were,

most certainly, the first to shock my heart back into life.

From the first infatuation, right up to the simple appreciation

when you were old enough to drive me in your car.

I felt a kindness that I had not been shown before;

you saw me without the glasses people had given you;

you smiled at me because you could;

and you sat next to me because you wanted to.

And though these are all simple things,

my hurt, lonely heart began to heal.

'Mistakes' will be made

Mistakes are an accompaniment to life,
that much is obvious,
but the worst comes from doing nothing
in anticipation of their arrival.

Who I used to be

He was starting to discover now that chaos had met the calm,

so little really mattered.

And though the silence scared him just as much as the noise,

there would always be tears, that much is for sure.

All the years he feared were wasted,

all the humiliation of past mistakes,

all the people he was scared of losing

and all those that were lost along the way,

they were all just bits and pieces;

worries in a hurry to call themselves important.

And he was starting to discover

that however long the lethargy in low spirits lasted,

however much help he would have to ask for,

however high the highs were and however low the lows were,

he had done so well and he would do so much better.

He just had to stop starting at the clock

and handling his heart with harshness

and just live.

Before Love is peace

I have spent most of my life craving the company of others,
but more recently, it is a remote island
and the promise of myself,
that has been calling my name.

Lighter

You were a candle I could not help
but to keep burning myself on,
the naked flame my hand would brush over
to get that sweet fleeting adrenaline of pain
and now I have escaped,
I can say
that I still savour the taste
from a safe distance.

As though first sight was a real thing

I always come back to you,

but I have yet to find the proper words

to define the poetry that pulls me toward

your love's mooring.

There are few souls that have seduced my own

so suddenly as yours did upon the meeting

of our eyes and yet my pen does not write of you

quite as much as the others.

I simply sit at my desk with my pen perched atop my notepad

and become too distracted by a picture of us;

by a feeling that I can remember, that I can almost feel

brimming through the fallen light of the photo,

as if the photo is the poem itself.

Every glance is another ticket to fall all over again;

another invite to experience the excitement of

your vibrant alignment with my silent euphoria.

Etymology

You're still a little bit of a mystery to me,

a word I know that occasionally

sounds different on the tongue.

A song that is objectively beautiful

but holds a note I cannot quite hear.

You, a woman of wonder,

of energy and simple fascination,

of happiness and pain combined

that makes me smile,

and who says it has to be anymore complicated

than that fact?

If only

If only I could have seen all of this at 15,
the beauty may just have taken all of my tears.

Touch

Bodies on a train,

the side of both their arms touch softly as the tracks

rock them against each other.

A breeze rolls in from the open window

and they both shiver

and throw a momentary glance at each other

and so begins this cuffing seasons first victims:

solo souls waiting for someone to share their heart with.

But what happens past the Christmas jeer?

when the harsh winter chill tests their intentions,

will their hands still touch come valentines?

or will they shiver on, knowing the cold

was never the issue.

Instagram

I must admit,

I lost my discipline the other day

and wandered across your page,

noticed your happiness: A new man,

a new life, for all purposes.

And I smiled, because while I felt disappointed in myself

for stalking your social media,

I was happy to discover you were living a life

that I always wanted for you.

And through all the momentary madness,

at the end of it all, you were a beautiful soul

with the potential for so much more

but with too much holding you back,

and I don't know if I was one of those too,

but I am happy either way that you made it.

Baggy jumper

Perfume is a perfect piece of persona
until it is found ground into the fabric
of forgotten jumpers.
I grab one from the cupboard
and lift it over my head and get a whiff;
a swift reminder that love was born of the senses, too.

Nothing ends

It never ended;
you just took different paths.

How do you feel now?

I love to read old poems

and remember just how much perspectives change.

I still ask the sky to keep an eye on you.

I hope it still shows you the stars

The First Dance

It has taken me many years to understand
the worlds lessons in loves,
but I learnt a great one from you/
It is strange to think I have only just realised
that what was once a reason for my heart to flutter
was also a moment never to be forgotten
And that this isn't about what ifs,
nr regretting not stumbling upon it earlier.
This is about the night when the DJ changed the tempo
and you came over and asked me if I'd look to join you
and we were two teenagers stumbling into a slow dance,
me holding you but too tall for it not to look a little clumsy,
a little too clumsy for it ever to be smooth anyway.
Some Elton John song soundtracking the moment,
my Dad somewhere in the background,
beaming, finally proud.
and a smattering of other dancing duos
but of course, it felt as if we were the main act;
a spotlight following our every stammered step.

Sometimes I stay quiet

You gave me immeasurable love and laughter
as we sang at the top of our lungs.
Something told me then that I would never find the words,
but to have you in my life was more than enough for me.

Autumn

I find comfort in falling leaves,

it proves that sometimes everything falls

but that it does not mean to say

that it was not

meant

to be.

A duo destined.

I remember being a child,

picking petals off of daffodils heads

and hoping when I reached the last,

I would smile and say "she Loves me".

And then I wasn't a child anymore,

and it wasn't daffodil petals but your sunflower speech

that sank me, and I smiled and said "I Love her".

I have been searching the nibs of my pens

to find a way to write of us,

but how do you translate something

that was already living poetry?

So I stopped asking the ink and began to pick apart the pieces

of my heart, that much like the petals,

had been ripped to the side, deciding if Love was real or not,

and they came together, a puzzle of past,

and spelt this song:

You were not a drug, nor magic -

you were the organ that kept me alive.

I am not religious, but I saw the pride of God in you.

I hung on your words like to miss a second was a tragedy

and I searched your eyes for the way they glared into mine

and heard as my chest imploded

with the weight of such almighty beating.

I cannot fathom the feeling in retrospect,

so overwhelming and enormous;

You were the war and the flag of surrender;

You were words that, once they have fallen out of the mouth,

leave it feeling empty.

anything I do now feels like nothing

but a shadow to such sensation,

and perhaps the collapse of such intense fire is inevitable

but I know that Love is an undefined thing,

and even if I find someone who replaces

the state of being you placed me in,

there will always be the tattoo of every mark you left.

And I guess it is because ours was a chemistry

that lit a flame without ever connecting.

It was science that saw me stuck to your soul,

and I believe, whatever happened in between

our two lost atoms,

te were meant to be for a time in life,

and we were, of some sort, a duo to be decorated.

And so, though I still don't know what to call you

and still get the urge to call you,

and know if I were to ever see you again,

I would fly back in time to when I could hear your voice

without my chest shattering like a window after

too many rocks thrown at its face,

I will watch our boat float down the river,

two hearts that did not know how to hold each other,

and I will wave goodbye with just a single tear,

knowing our time was here and then was gone

and that for some, that is all that was meant to be.

And I can see that now,

as much as it tears me apart, I can finally start again.

and when someone arrives with an outstretched hand,

I will not turn them away in fear of the end.

I will welcome them,

show them around the walls of this crumbling house

and let life do what it must, for better, for worse.

I will always be grateful for the time spent

and the lessons learnt with you.

nothing has ever thrilled me nor broken me

quite like it.

On the sixth floor

On the sixth floor with thirteen books and my blue laptop

and the poison of three energy drinks

coursing through my veins

and dark, baggy eyes to match,

I took a look at that stupid blank page and almost cried

at the lack of 3000 words on the history of orientalism.

So I reached out to my phone and found your name:

"In library. Come join me so we can die of exhaustion together xx"

you laughed and said you were already a floor below me

and not just that, but you had a bag of those mouth-watering

chocolate doughnuts I loved so much.

And you arrived and we were just two tired students

in the library at 10:23pm,

giving each other the energy we needed.

Your smile, invigorating.

Your mind, revitalising.

And every word you said

restored my brain to some semblance of normality.

I think I only managed 300 words in the end,

but with chocolate stained cheeks and eyes with new light,

I was happy to have been in that building that was too big

for that time of night and to have shared it with you.

To have been buried under the weight of too many essays

and too many dreams

and to have shared it with you.

A fun distraction

It was all so quick

hat I barely had time to remember anything,

such that my mind took the default route

and called it forgettable.

And though I imagine the stars never cared to 'ship' us

and no earthquakes shattered when our two lips touched,

I do think of the small moments from time to time.

Like the night we first kissed

and how our thumbs stroked over the other

and all the romanticism of our first meeting

and me ignoring the warnings from a friend;

It felt thrilling to be a little reckless,

and you were a perfect distraction

from the mundanity

of a cautious life.

It felt meteoric

I don't know if I was in Love or in awe,

I just know the feeling was profound.

A spot reserved

I have Loved a great many,
but been in Love only a couple times
and I have no doubt that
you sit at the top, my darling.

I *needed that*

You told me you loved me more than anything in the world
and I looked into your eyes,
those wide wonders,
and for once
believed what I heard.

I hope my gift gives you joy

I hope you never lost the cup I gave you.

I hope you sip from the rim and enjoy the hot chocolate.

I hope you think of me

and do not think of anything other than the good times.

I hope you drink to the memory,

I hope you smile

and are not for sad the loss,

but are so divinely inspired that we ever met.

Grace of Living

For every sweet word you uttered

and every look of kindness,

I found a reason to believe

I was worthy of Love.

Part 2: 6 personal essays on love

Essay 1: Open To Everything

If you've read this book chronologically, you will now be arriving at a slightly different part of this journey. Here, I want to just talk to you. Keep the poetry of the past 3 sections in the back of your mind and let's talk about the culmination of these elements; talk about the reason this book – in all its romantic optimism - exists. Talk about how its reason for being can give you a reason to unlearn and re-invent everything you know about Love. About the feeling, about the term and about the finality of it's application.

So, let's talk.

Some of my friends and family might read this book and think "Well, what does he know? He's been single for 26 years, bar the occasional date or complication" and it's a question I've been asking myself. It was the question that stopped me writing this book, despite the fact that I felt it's call-to-action scratching under my skin. I felt it's need for creation at several points in my life because I knew I had a story to tell, despite not having the romantic 'luck' that so many others have. In fact, rather *because* of this exact fact, I knew I had a story to tell. Yet it never came together as a tangible, digestible, understanding until a couple of years ago. Obviously, it wasn't just a case of a light bulb shining above my head and everything falling into place. Of course not. It was 2 years of learning, of transforming, of challenging my pre-determined ideals and education of Love, romance, friendship and feeling.

I had become exhausted, had pulled the last straw from the hay bail and was now just looking back on a collapsed structure of romantic failures, embarrassments and cringey attachments. At least that's how I used to look back on them, and here is one of my largest lessons. Here is what the book is all about. I am not writing a book on how to stay in Love, how to be the best partner in the world or even how to find the right person for you. How Love Begins is about understanding… well… how Love begins. It is about discovering a new way to review the situations of the past and feel inspired by their beauty in such a way that you don't give up on Love as a whole, as a concept. But this is easier said than done. Why? Because it's not always easy to see the beauty in situations that have passed, as more often than not they've passed for a very good reason. They've passed because things have become hostile or toxic or the Love has simply dissipated or the Love was always one sided.

It's a complex topic that lends itself to an infinite number of outcomes, but there lies part of its beauty and the key to understanding it: there is an infinite number of outcomes. Infinite because there is always someone new and with someone new, even when it feels like the same string of events, the same situation, it's not. There are granular changes, there are fundamental emotional changes. There are elements that make it new. It's important to understand this because if you are exhausted or stressed and you are realising that you are in the middle of watching Love fall apart again, you're gonna give up. However, if you are watching, still upset but aware that there are differences in the way events have unfolded or in the seams of their being, then you are aware that Love is still evolving and changing. And if Love can evolve, then we still have an endless amount to learn. When we are aware of the minor changes, we can no longer confidently say "I know what's going to happen" because we don't.

Whatsmore is that if we believe we know what will happen, we will breathe that energy into the world and encourage it to come true. Whereas if we set no expectation or pressure, then we are telling the world and the universe that we are open to everything. When we are open to everything, then we are opening the door to the greatest things. Think of all the times you've looked back on "almost Loves" and "if only Loves" and thought about what could be different. Usually, timing does its own thing, if it didn't happen, there's probably a reason. But at the same time, if you constantly tell yourself that you are not deserving of a true Love or when the universe presents you with someone for you, you say "no, I am not worthy", then the universe will have no choice but to send you someone that is not right for you. To really be Loved in the way you want, in the way you deserve, you have to be open to everything. Open to the idea that you are worthy of everything good. Open to the idea that your true Love may not be what you think it is. Open to the patience that may be essential. Open to the concept of being open. Only then will you see more than you ever saw before.

I really want to stress that being open in this way is not about forced intention. I am not asking you to open your eyes to things and tell them that they *must* love everything they come in contact with. Being open in the way I describe, is just about giving in to what is already there. In fact, by that definition, it is the very opposite of forced intention. It is instinct, it is freedom from rigidity and acceptance of life's fluidity of motion. To finish this book and announce to yourself, "I will be open to everything" is to, in the same breath, declare a new trust for the signals in your body and mind. To be open to everything is to stop closing doors that scare you.

Essay 2: Pure Love

One of the most precious Loves of all that many of us misunderstand or, often, fail to truly encounter is a *pure* Love. Pure Love has a perception, perhaps, of being virginal. Of being vanilla or only attributed to those of certain personalities. We imagine purity as something stripped bare and devoid of anything of a modern society. Do I agree? Well, yes and no. The way I refer to 'Pure Love' is a Love that, in whatever form or regarding whatever relation, comes from an undiluted core of being. A Pure Love that is so in abundance that it spills forth in buckets. It is all-powerful and demands to be spoken. In fact, it does not demand, it simply just *is*. It lives as a testament to interpersonal gratitude; an ode to awe. It is a Love that feeds the mutual self.

The reason so many of us forget to recognise it is because sometimes we are so busy with life that when we share a connection that is fundamentally natural, we take our time in realising how wonderful a thing it is. In that time, there is actually a beauty as well because it is organic, it is moulded by the most destined order of events. The distinction, though, is when we fail to accept it as opposed to simply acknowledging it. When we do not acknowledge it, sometimes it is life's way of turning our heads and saying "no, this isn't for you yet but it will be at some point". But when we acknowledge it and choose not to explore it or to submit to it or even to accept that it exists, that is when we do ourselves a disservice. That is when we invite chaos and confusion. That is when our bodies and our minds will cry out for our cooperation and we have a duty to listen.

That Pure Love that we so often underestimate will arrive as an invite. It will arrive and ask you gently to listen, to ask questions, to feel it's beating rhythm. It will not stomp its feet and jump in front of you to get your attention, it will simply hold your hand and attempt to guide you. But in order to reach that self-peace and that purest of Loves, you have to hold it back, you have to say "yes, please show me the way; be my guide" or it will just walk away. It may come back but it will walk away. You see, Pure Love is Love in collaboration. Collaboration between you, another soul and the universe. It is connecting with a higher state of appreciation for life and each other. It is tapping into an undesignated, undefined area of the body, mind and energy that inspires an overwhelming and profound feeling. It is then translating that grandiose emotion into words, into comprehension, into a journey in motion.

Pure Love is something that varies between person to person, but in essence, it is the ability to throw everything you know under the bus and just be completely under the spell of it. It is grabbing hold of it, but not letting it slip easily away. It is not being dependent on it, but letting it support you. It is not avoiding the tide, but also not drowning in it. It is a perfect balance that it is more about finding it and accepting it, than crafting or moulding it, or believing that it can be created from force. A Pure Love is a Love, undiluted by expectation and uplifted by softness of heart.

Essay 3: Love is Love

One thing that I do know about Love is that it does not judge and it is, most certainly, not exclusive to a select few. Love is a right, a freedom of being. It is the natural essence of our existence and that applies to absolutely every person, animal and being on this planet and in our known universe. For years, some have tried to take this away from our fellow earth siblings by denying them this right, by vilifying their brand of Love, by refusing to accept a Love that does not look like theirs as still worthy. But what these people speak of is not Love. At least not in its true form, not in its pure form, not in any form that should be taken seriously.

They speak of a construct of society. That isn't Love. That is a rule, and Love, by nature, is rebellious to the rules of society. What they speak of is a label applied to those of a majority dominance in order to sustain their dominance, to sustain their hierarchy of pretension. They will try to convince you that Love is simple, that it only wears 2 colours, that it can be described in 1 go. That, if you do not feel it, you should be converted until you do.

Let me make something very clear, reader: even they know what they speak of is ancient history. They know that they speak only from envy, fear of change and of confusion. But do not let their own internal grief and attachment to stale ideals define or degrade your own. Whoever you are, whoever you find yourself falling in Love with: you are beautiful, you are whole and you are a piece of nature that has designed itself in excellence and intention. Love is natural, however it decides to arrive. Love is being unapologetically true. Love is land that is to be discovered. Love is leaving some fluidity of being to understand who you Love is who you Love. Love is being born the way you are and knowing that you deserve the same feeling, the same beauty, the same respect, the same unimaginable satisfaction, no matter what.

I do not know you or your circumstance. I do not know your identity or what Love looks like to you but I want you to know that every part of this book is equally for you as it is for anyone else. I want you to know that if you carry Love inside of you, if you feel it, then that's all that matters. Life can be hard and people can be cruel, but Love exists and that's enough to keep us living. That's enough to connect us all. That's enough to allow anyone on this planet to smile and scream at the top of their lungs "I love and I belong."

Essay 4: Love Is Also You

Self Love is not everything we see online, it's not the thousands of articles written on it every day. No, that's a version of it and I have gladly contributed to this for almost 6 years. What we tell you is a guide to a limitless exploration of self. But what we all seem to forget - both us as self-help writers and you as our readers - is that Self Love is not just this Love that is an appreciation or a liking of ourselves. Like, you CAN also fall in love with yourself. I'm talking, totally infatuated with an element of your being, utterly in awe of your talent, completely grateful for your existence. It is confidence without ego, it is understanding that the strength and loyalty of our heart also belongs to us. Whatsmore is that Love is not just us because we are in Love with ourselves, it is also just defined by our existence. By simply being alive today, you are Love. You are a vessel of Love, you are a divine receptor for Love, you are a scientist of Love. You are Love and by result, you are worthy of Love, too. Because how can Love ever be unworthy of a thing like itself?

You have the ability to create things, to give things, to receive, to believe and to realise. You have the potential to show yourself what you are capable of every single day. You are Love, made to last. You are a beating heart without a caged rib. You are the sunshine on a french beach. You are splendid in nature. You are

Love. I understand some of this might sound absolutely ridiculous or like utter hocus pocus, but just take a nibble of this concept and grow it. Think of yourself as Love, itself, and figure out what that means in your life. My definition here and the wording I use works for me but it might be completely different for you and that's fine. But to take even a morsel of what I have suggested here and to explore is to get a taste of something we haven't been taught enough in life. We haven't been taught how to find that Love inside of ourselves or to define it without the presence of someone else in its equation. However old you are, you have the chance to do that now. You have the chance to explore Love as a concept devoted to you and by extension, apply it to Love shared. Something as authentic and personalised as that helps us to understand exactly what it is we need to be satisfied. And remember, contentment is not satisfaction. Satisfaction is giving yourself what you *need* and what you *deserve,* Love.

Essay 5: Love as Unrequited

A lot of this ties into Essay 4, but I want to apply it to one of the more heartbreaking situations within Love: when it's unrequited. Now, a significant portion of these poems were about Loves that were not reciprocated, either partially or fully, but you will notice that I still give them the same sensual, celebrated existence. They still stand tall within this book as a gift of greatness. That's because it's no different from any other love. What we call unrequited Love is still returned to us. It may not be returned by the person we Love, but it will be returned by the energy created by its fire.

Love, in any form, is food for the body, mind and spirit and yet we still reduce unrequited Love to something unimportant or small. Two of the strongest Loves that I mentioned in this book were unspoken or unrequited but they were an exceptional creation within me and a powerful memory. So let's dig into a for-instance, shall we?

Picture the scene: you meet someone new, you get on really well and there seems to be an attraction. You spend a little time building up the courage and eventually you tell them how you feel. They don't feel the same - argh, you're crushed! But how do you respond? How do your heart, mind and body react? Most of us might distance ourselves from that person to allow ourselves to heal or we might erase that first memory from our minds to ignore the fact of it's being. We might even feel ashamed or humiliated and feel as though we can never be the same around that person. I know that I've felt and done every single one of those things but I don't anymore, for a very good reason: we're all human and we all Love.

Think about it, in the creation of friendship or of an initial bond, there is a moment where you do not know each other. There is a moment when the energy between you is a mystery and the dots have not been connected. All you know is how you feel. Nothing about that is bad. Nothing about that is anything to be ashamed or humiliated of. In fact, I've come to feel intoxicated by it, to feel so amazed and fascinated by it that I've created an entire book on the subject. The start of everything is the most incredible feeling and an exciting moment in any of our lives - we should treasure it as such! Your brain is inflamed by the idea of another person. You are drinking in all this information about them and becoming steadily inebriated by the promise of it all. The sheer fact that an experience like that can exist is something that should be shouted from the rooftops, whether they return Love to the fullest extent or not. In fact, some of the best friendships can be created this way because you're spending more time *listening*, more time *wondering*, more time being utterly *interested*.

Whatsmore is that you need these rejections to get a better understanding of who you truly need and who is a better match for you. Don't do what we were told to do as men and just keep asking until they give up (grim), take the rejection, celebrate the initial fire and move on. Sometimes, it's not the right time, sometimes it's not the right person and rejections allow us to realise this. They allow us to look back on the feeling and figure out what it was about that person that inspired something so profound inside of us. Equally, in that retrospective look, we can sometimes realise that it was more of an admiration than a Love and that rejection has already saved us the awkwardness of a later realisation.

It all feels very complicated and unrequited Love can hurt just as much as a breakup, but understand that this is just one person amongst thousands you will meet in your entire life. They are a beautiful element now and they will always be a great memory, but when the right person comes along and you both share a love, you will be thankful for everything that led to that moment. You will be thankful that you never gave up asking people. You will be thankful that you changed your perception. You will be thankful that you loved so many to reach that one and you will be thankful that you said anything, for the sake of knowing the answer.

Love as unrequited is Love as precious as all.

Essay 6: Its All Love

Perhaps you could call this my concluding thesis of sorts. The crescendo to this symphonic exploration of Love. The lawyer making his pretentious final statements for his onlooking jury to make their own judgements based on the evidence.

In short, it really is All Love.

We have spent too long fussing about the categories of Love, of whether unrequited Love is still Love, of whether a fleeting summer "fling" is as true as a 10 year marriage. We have become so concerned with discussing what counts as Love and what counts as a "great Love" or a "true Love" that we have failed to take stock of what Love actually means to us. What does it feel like? What happens when a few years pass and we look back? What happens if we try our best to attach a positive perspective on it all? What if we told ourselves that Love had no name? No face? No body or Being? What if all the brick walls of everything we once believed was to be shattered? Bulldozed down like some old cottages in replace for a modern complex of flats?

Does Love become more interesting then? And, if so, why wait? Why not take the moment and make Love something hopeful again. Make it beautiful. Make it exciting. Make it thrilling. Make it everything we wanted the films to inspire. Make it yours. Make it exceptional. Make it broad and varied and make it what you will.

Because it's all Love. And if you really look back at how Love begins, you'll see that. I know that Love can be an exhausting and painful experience, too. I know that after enough knockbacks, it becomes so difficult to ever believe that what you want and need will come true. I know that even knowing who it is you want or the things you need can be just as impossible as learning algebra for the first time and wondering why letters exist in math. I know that at some point in this book, you have probably rolled your eyes at the sentimentality of many of these poems. I know that some of the things I speak of can be hard to comprehend or to think of as anything but spiritualistic poppycock. But I also know that you picked this book for a reason. I know that sometimes, we just need a little reminder of how beautiful Love can be in order to give ourselves the excuse to try again. I know that when we get sad after a breakup, we eat junk food and watch any Romance we can, either to dream of its perceived simplicity or to relive what we've already felt. Well, here's your excuse. Here's your reminder. Here's your reasoning. Pick yourself up, go to therapy if it feels like it hurts enough, and then remind yourself why you try each time.

Remind yourself that Love is one of the greatest things any of us can feel and remind yourself that it's all Love and if that is true, there is little to be afraid of. Remind yourself that you are Love, that you are worthy of Love, that you are allowed to reinvent it. Remind yourself that this book was written by someone who has had far more heartbreaks than anything positive. Remind yourself that time can be short, that to not speak of Love is to not know if it is true or shared and to know of one Love is not to know of them all. Remind yourself that even when you think you've been through it all, there's so much more beauty to be found, if only you would find the courage to start again.

About The Author

Liam Xavier is an Anglo-Carribean writer, performer and producer who has spent several years honing his style in a bid to translate a life of confusion, trauma, beauty and growth. He has bylines at several online publications, such as Thought Catalog, Be A Light, The Mighty, The Unwritten and more, garnering thousands of views with each article. He co-runs a theatre company with fellow writer and performer, Lauren Williams (City Heart, 2021) and uses his writing, theatre and performance to raise awareness of social injustices and mental health issues. He also recently created TCTW, an online publication devoted to using a fascination with research to create articles and infographics to raise awareness of various causes and issues. With TCTW, he hopes to build a resource centre for those that want to learn more about the world and to give a voice to those that struggle to express their opinion correctly. Liam, if you couldn't tell, is not satisfied with doing just one thing, but many.

Instagram: @liamxavierwrites @wiflen_theatre @wordstctw
Twitter: @liamxavier95 @WilflenT @tctw12
Facebook: @liamxavier95 @WilflenTheatre @factstctw
Website: www.liamxavier.co.uk, www.wilflentheatre.co.uk, www.tochangetheworld.co.uk